# Animals Adapt

by Lian Wu

D1708729

Glenview, Illinois • Boston, Massachusetts • Mesa, Arizona
Shoreview, Minnesota • Upper Saddle River, New Jersey

Animals adapt for many reasons.
Why do they adapt? Animals adapt to solve problems.

Animals adapt to where they live and to the weather.

Animals adapt in order to survive.

---

**adapt:** to change to fit different conditions

Plants and animals adapt to their environment. Lions adapted and have very strong teeth. This helps them eat prey such as zebras. But zebras also adapted. They have strong legs to help them run away from lions.

---

**environment:** the world around people, plants, and animals

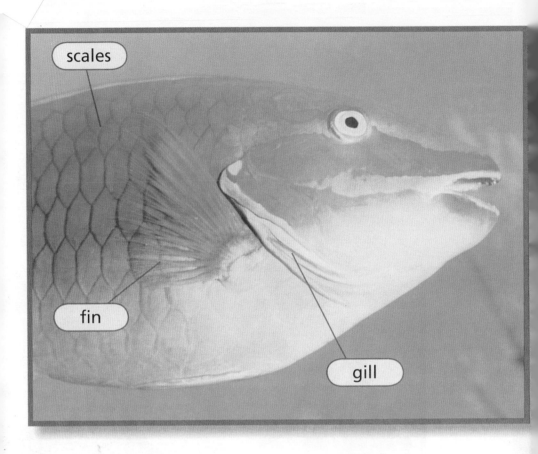

scales

fin

gill

### Fish Adapt

Like other animals, fish adapted to survive. But fish adapted to live in an underwater environment. They need to move and breathe in water. Fish cannot survive on land. So they developed different body parts: fins, gills, and scales.

The fish uses its fins to swim.

Fish developed fins to swim in water. They also developed gills to breathe in water. Fish take water into their gills to breathe. The gills take air out of the water for the fish's body. Fish have scales instead of skin to protect against the water.

---

**scales:** small, flat, bony pieces that cover a fish's body

tail

fur

## Beavers Adapt

Beavers live in rivers or lakes. Their thick fur help keep them warm. Their long, wide tails helps beavers swim. Beavers also have strong teeth that help them eat the bark of trees.

**bark:** rough, hard part of the wood on the outside of tree trunks

lodge

A beaver builds a home.

Beavers live in lodges. They build their lodges with twigs, branches, and leaves. Every year, beavers add new material to their homes. A beaver's lodge has an entrance at the bottom. Beavers swim in and out of the entrance.

shell

### Turtles Adapt

Turtles can walk on dry land. They are one of the slowest land animals. But turtles adapted in order to survive. Their shells became very hard. A turtle can protect itself by hiding in its hard shell.

Turtles can swim under the water. But they cannot breathe under water. The lungs of turtles adapted. They do not need air often. A turtle comes to the surface when it needs air.

---

**surface:** the top of the ground or the water

ears

## Rabbits Adapt

Rabbits are very small animals. But they have adapted to help stay safe. The ears of rabbits became very long. This helps them hear when a predator is near.

**predator:** an animal that hunts and eats other animals

legs

Rabbits also have powerful legs. Their strong legs help them run away. When they hear another animal coming, they run away fast. Many predators cannot catch a quick rabbit.

Think about the animals you see everyday. Now think about the environment they live in. How do you think these animals adapted in order to survive?